I0407584

TABLE OF CONTENTS

INTRODUCTION

Who is a Professional Makeup Artist?

    What kind of Personality you should have?

    Reflect on your Makeup Skills and Services

    Learn how to do Makeup Correctly

    Keep Improving your Portfolio

What does a Makeup Artist do?

    Duties and Responsibilities

    Types of Makeup Artists

What It Means To Work as A Makeup Artist

    Working for free

    You don't work the regular five times a week

    You have odd hours – early days and late nights

    Clients may expect too much from you as artist

    Tired is not an excuse. You may have to travel a lot

    Financial issues

    Becoming a makeup artist can be expensive

How to become a professional makeup artist

    Enroll in a makeup program at cosmetology school

    Build your portfolio with makeup photos and other visuals

    Be social with clients and hair stylists

Learn new makeup styles and trends
How to Become a Makeup Artist
    Getting Started as a Makeup Artist
    Learn Essential Methods & Techniques
    Gain Experience & Professional Connections
How to become a makeup artist. Top do's & don'ts
    General Advice
    Do's & Don'ts
A Successful Makeup Artist
    Practice Makeup on Friends and Family
    Work on Your Portfolio
    Connect With Fellow MUAs & to the Market
    Learn How to Advertise Your Service On Social Media
    Get Trained and Receive a Diploma From a Makeup School
    Additional Tips on How You Can Become a Makeup Artist
More Steps to Become a Professional Makeup Artist
    Choose Your Niche
    Practice Hard
    Get Formal Education
    Create a Portfolio
    Market Yourself
    Be Professional
How to Become a Professional Makeup Artist
    Things You Should Know
    Developing Your Skills
    Getting Education and Professional Experience
    Creating a Portfolio
    Building Your Career
Tips to become a successful makeup artist

Get Enrolled In A Good Place
Practice
Figure Out The Best and Bad
Networking Is Important
Learn the New Trend
Always Have Your Secrets
Don't Overdo It!!
Respect Your Job

INTRODUCTION

A makeup artist is a professional who applies cosmetics and beauty products to enhance the appearance of individuals, typically for television, film, theater, or special events. The primary goal of a makeup artist is to use their skills and knowledge to create a specific look that meets the client's needs and enhances their natural features. Makeup artists use various techniques, such as contouring, highlighting, and shading, to accentuate facial features, create illusions, and bring out the desired look.

Makeup artists work with a wide range of clients, from actors and models to everyday people who want to look their best for special occasions. They need to have excellent communication skills and be able to understand their client's needs and preferences. They also need to be knowledgeable about different skin types and tones, as well as the various types of makeup and products available. Additionally, they must keep up-to-date with the latest trends in the makeup industry and be able to adapt their techniques to meet the demands of different clients and projects.

WHO IS A PROFESSIONAL MAKEUP ARTIST?

A professional makeup artist uses cosmetics products on the human body to increase beauty through makeup skills. The role of a professional makeup artist is challenging as they make our favorite style. They have the ability and skill to make a unique look completely different, most of the time beautiful, sometimes dangerous, as per the requirement.

WHAT KIND OF PERSONALITY YOU SHOULD HAVE?

No difficulty you are going to be presented to different companies, industries, brands, etc. when you come into the makeup industry and going to meet a number of people and with whom you will be working. Therefore, you should have a personality makes you more active and helps you to stay in this field for a long time. Even if you start your career as a wedding makeup artist you must have proper skills and services to be the Best Bridal Makeup Artist in Delhi.

REFLECT ON YOUR MAKEUP SKILLS AND SERVICES

After completing the makeup artist course from makeup school, you have received enough makeup skills and you are ready to work, but you cannot call yourself a professional of the industry. You need to find out what you are good at and the skills that you need to work on.

LEARN HOW TO DO MAKEUP CORRECTLY

Having certification and some experience is important when you begin your career as a professional makeup artist. Improve your skills as much as possible through makeup classes. Conventional education isn't necessary for many artists around the world. But it can surely help and put you ahead from other artists who don't have any professional makeup course.

KEEP IMPROVING YOUR PORTFOLIO

You have to continue trying to build a more suitable portfolio by increasing the capacity of people you are working with — superior photographers, lovelier models with better skin, etc. Also, make sure that the shoots you are doing add to your portfolio. For example, do wedding shoots, if you are trying to be a bridal makeup artist, a fitness model shoot help you. Offer to help student films, if you're looking to do a film, and continue to improve.

WHAT DOES A MAKEUP ARTIST DO?

Makeup artists play an essential role in enhancing the appearance of individuals and creating looks that can transform an actor into a character, a model into a work of art, or a bride into a stunning vision on her wedding day. They have the skills and knowledge to accentuate an individual's best features and camouflage any perceived flaws, allowing their clients to feel confident and beautiful. In many industries, such as film, television, and fashion, makeup artists are an integral part of the creative team, helping to bring the director or designer's vision to life.

DUTIES AND RESPONSIBILITIES

The duties and responsibilities of a makeup artist may vary depending on the industry they work in, but here are some common tasks and responsibilities:

• Consult with clients: The first step in a makeup artist's job is to consult with clients and understand their preferences, skin type, and the occasion. They need to have excellent communication skills to understand clients' needs and make suggestions.

• Apply makeup: Once the client's needs are understood, the makeup artist applies makeup products to enhance their natural features, cover up blemishes, and create a desired look. This may include foundation, blush, eyeshadow, eyeliner, lipstick, and more.

• Match skin tone: It's important for makeup artists to understand how to match skin tone to the right foundation, concealer, and other products. They also need to understand how different lighting and cameras may affect how the makeup appears on the skin.

• Maintain cleanliness: A makeup artist must maintain cleanliness in their work area and equipment. They need to ensure their brushes and other tools are sanitized properly to avoid spreading infections.

• Stay up to date on trends: A makeup artist should be aware of the latest trends and techniques in the industry. They should be able to suggest new ideas to clients, and stay updated on the latest product innovations.

• Work with different skin types: A makeup artist should be familiar with different skin types and tones. They should know how to apply makeup to different skin textures, whether it's oily, dry, or combination skin.

• Work on different occasions: Makeup artists may work on different occasions, such as weddings, fashion shows, photoshoots, or movie sets. They should be able to adapt their makeup style to suit the occasion.

• Understand special effects makeup: In some industries, such as theater or movie productions, makeup artists need to be able to create special effects makeup, such as aging or injuries, to make the characters look realistic.

TYPES OF MAKEUP ARTISTS

There are several different types of makeup artists, each with their own specialties and areas of expertise. Here are some of the most common types of makeup artists:

• Bridal makeup artist: These makeup artists specialize in creating beautiful, natural-looking makeup for brides on their wedding day. They may also work with the bridal party, such as bridesmaids, mothers of the bride and groom, and other family members.

• Fashion makeup artist: These makeup artists work in the fashion industry, creating bold and avant-garde looks for runway shows, editorial photo shoots, and advertising campaigns.

• Celebrity makeup artist: These makeup artists work with celebrities, creating looks for red carpet events, movie premieres, and other high-profile appearances.

• Special effects makeup artist: These makeup artists specialize in creating prosthetics, scars, and other effects to make actors look like different characters. They may work in film, television, or theater.

• Editorial makeup artist: These makeup artists work in the publishing industry, creating makeup looks for fashion magazines, catalogs, and other publications.

• Cosmetic makeup artist: These makeup artists work for cosmetic companies, such as MAC, Sephora, and Estée Lauder, demonstrating how to use their products and creating makeup looks for clients.

• Theatrical makeup artist: These makeup artists specialize in creating makeup looks for theater productions, including dramatic stage makeup and character makeup.

WHAT IT MEANS TO WORK AS A MAKEUP ARTIST

Makeup artists seem to live the ultimate glamorous and glitzy life. With opportunities to travel all over the world, work backstage on models who walk the runway, apply makeup on the faces of famous celebrities and many more, becoming a professional makeup artist seems relatively easy and straightforward. However, there's more to it than simply booking clients and showing up at the right location and time.

The journey to becoming a successful professional makeup artist is not effortless; it takes an unbelievable amount of hard work and perseverance to achieve the level of expertise that most people are looking for in a makeup artist. Unknown to many, beneath all of the different colors and makeup products reveal an artist who had to sacrifice many things in order to bring out the natural beauty of others and help them to feel confident everyday. After going through countless hours of practicing, makeup artist don't start their career the instant they graduate and receive their certification.

Below are some situations that you may run into when first starting out as a makeup artist. Although these will most likely happen, they should not discourage you from pursuing the career that you are passionate about. Pushing through will make it all worth it in the end!

• You may have to work for free at first

• Working everyday is not guaranteed

• Your days start early and end late

• Clients may not love every makeup look

• Traveling can be a bit of a hassle

• Money may not come in as easily

• Being a makeup artist is an investment

It's never that easy. But just because it may seem challenging doesn't mean that it's unattainable. Even though it might take longer than you had originally planned, there's not doubt that you're going to make it. All it takes is persistence and a little bit of patience.

WORKING FOR FREE

Much like internships, you may have to work for free at first in order to gain the necessary experience. Although there may not be a lot of paying opportunities, you will learn many skills while being on-the-job. You may have to exchange your services before you are able to start charging others.

Nevertheless, you will have the chance to build and add to your portfolio, and you may even have the opportunity to have your work published either in print or online. This will make you seem as a more credible artist and you will soon have clients asking to book you.

YOU DON'T WORK THE REGULAR FIVE TIMES A WEEK

As much as this sounds like a dream, working as a freelance makeup artist can be quite difficult. Although you get to set your own schedule, sometimes that may be because you might not have many bookings coming in. Yes, it can be wonderful to have as many rest days as you want, but rest days also mean no projects or clients; which leads to less income being generated. But you can make the most of your free time by networking with professionals in the same industry.

Making connections with photographers, models and other professional makeup artists can lead to invaluable opportunities to help you achieve your career goals. It's always important to remember that networking doesn't just serve you, but is a mutually beneficial activity. You never know when your skills and resources can prove to be helpful to others in your professional circle.

YOU HAVE ODD HOURS – EARLY DAYS AND LATE NIGHTS

If you're not looking to work the typical 9-5 desk job, then having a career in makeup artistry may be your calling. However, this doesn't necessarily mean that you'll have an easy schedule. In fact, you may have to sacrifice a whole day or two depending on your client or project. Due to special occasions or demanding clients, you may have to start the makeup process way before the event starts, and you may even have to stay all the way until the end. You may have no choice but to go along, as it can hurt your reputation to say no.

CLIENTS MAY EXPECT TOO MUCH FROM YOU AS ARTIST

When you are booked by a client, they are putting all of their trust in you to deliver a look that they will fall in love with, which can be quite nerve-wrecking for you. As you go through the makeup application, clients may question your choices and put a lot of pressure on you. Sooner or later, you're going to run into some difficult people.Some will be easy to please, while others may be more high-maintenance. In the end, they will all end up expecting nothing but the best from you. It doesn't hurt to ask your client what their preference is.

TIRED IS NOT AN EXCUSE. YOU MAY HAVE TO TRAVEL A LOT

Do you want to get out and see the world? Many people do, and a career in makeup artistry may offer just that. But there are always some cons to every situation. It can be tough having to travel longer than you would spend the time to finish your actual work.

You may get to travel to some amazing cities, but you might not even have the time to explore. Traveling through different time zones can upset your sleeping schedule, making it difficult to concentrate. However, if you're willing to go the extra mile, your wanderlust could serve you well as your adaptability will build up an impressive reputation.

FINANCIAL ISSUES

You can make good money out of being a makeup artist, but this is usually after you have built up a clientele as well as other factors such as: your location, if you are able to do both hair and makeup, and your years of experience. As mentioned before, getting to a point where you can charge more for your services may take some time, but the amount you charge should reflect your talent as an artist. This means that you can never practice enough in order to get to where you need to go!

BECOMING A MAKEUP ARTIST CAN BE EXPENSIVE

Because you are a professional, you expected to have an array of high-quality makeup products. You know this by now, but makeup can be very pricy. You are also expected to know all the techniques behind creating a great look – both old and new. This is why attending a makeup school to amplify your knowledge and techniques, get a diploma to be certified, and lastly, get that generous discount to constantly update your professional makeup kit.

HOW TO BECOME A PROFESSIONAL MAKEUP ARTIST

Do you love experimenting with makeup? Are you obsessed with staying up to date on all the latest beauty trends? Turn your passion into a career as a professional makeup artist! You can with these five steps.

ENROLL IN A MAKEUP PROGRAM AT COSMETOLOGY SCHOOL

The only way to truly master your craft is with an education. That's where cosmetology school comes in! You'll learn the skills and techniques you need to find success in the beauty industry. It'll also help you prepare for the State Board exam so you can become a licensed professional and land the job you've always wanted. At beauty school, you'll meet instructors and peers and begin to build your network of contacts before you even finish your program.

BUILD YOUR PORTFOLIO WITH MAKEUP PHOTOS AND OTHER VISUALS

Just like any artist, your cosmetology portfolio showcases your talent and creativity. Use engaging visuals to highlight all that you can do. For a professional, high-quality look, make sure you take the best photos. Build your portfolio early on and upload it to your linkedin profile.

BE SOCIAL WITH CLIENTS AND HAIR STYLISTS

Makeup artists regularly interact with clients, hair stylists, and other members of a glam team, so you should be able to communicate and socialize well both in person and online. Social media is your digital platform for exhibiting your work and building your clientele. Get the word out to other industry professionals by connecting with beauty bloggers, YouTube gurus, and Instagram stars. And don't miss the opportunity to attend events and competitions to interact with live people in your profession.

Network with people in the makeup industry

In the beauty industry, it's all about who you know. Most of your work and clients will come from referrals, so your network is crucial. The more connections you have, the better your chances are of landing the job you've always wanted.

LEARN NEW MAKEUP STYLES AND TRENDS

Your education doesn't stop at graduation. The beauty industry is constantly changing with new trends growing in popularity each and every day. A true professional is always curious and learns all about the latest styles and techniques.

HOW TO BECOME A MAKEUP ARTIST

Professional makeup artists are some of the most in-demand artists in the entertainment industry today. If you have an artistic eye, a good sense of color, a love of makeup, and a passion for self-expression, this demanding field may be the right fit for you.

GETTING STARTED AS A MAKEUP ARTIST

Makeup artistry is a highly creative and interesting career that allows for artistic freedom and self-expression via a living canvas. This extremely competitive field demands that aspiring artists have plenty of experience, a strong work ethic, and connections to the performing arts/stage or entertainment industry.

A makeup artist is someone who knows how to use a wide variety of cosmetic techniques and processes to create beautiful scenes on the human body. This work should either enhance a subject's appearance, or in the more extreme sense, create imaginative characters and special effects for film, television, theater, and in photography. Currently, two main industries employ most makeup artists – cosmetic/fashion makeup and theatrical/film makeup.

Whatever path is chosen, both cosmetic and theatrical makeup artists must learn to how to work with the different lines and angles of the face and body, different lighting conditions, high definition cameras, and in many cases, a design team that may consist of directors, fashion designers and more. Each state has different requirements to become a certified makeup artist. Some require special licensing, while others may only require certain certifications. While a degree is not required for this career path, education will be beneficial depending on which area of makeup artistry you are interested in pursuing.

According to the US Bureau of Labor Statistics, makeup artists in theater and performance make a median wage of $44,310 per year. Professionals in the field with years of experience and a stellar reputation can make upwards of $115,000. The motion picture and video industries employ the highest levels of makeup artists, with personal care services, performing arts companies, and radio and television broadcasting companies following closely. It should also be noted, that you may have to go where the work is, as California, Nevada, and New York employ the most makeup artists in the US. But wages are highest in California, New York, and Georgia.

LEARN ESSENTIAL METHODS & TECHNIQUES

To become a successful makeup artist, a deep love for cosmetics and a passion to transform an art form is essential. If this is your desire, it is important that you work to learn about and continuously develop formal concepts, methods, theory, and techniques that are relevant to this creative field.Self-expression with makeup is something that humans have relied on for centuries, and as a makeup artist, you can create meaningful, frightful, clever, dramatic, and imaginative looks with makeup. The conception process allows makeup artists to come up the ideas that drive each piece of work. These concepts should serve as the underlying purpose or concept behind each finished face or body design. When you have a strong formal concept, you should be able to choose the right colors, application processes, and any accessories needed to enhance that design. As a makeup artist, you should also possess a clear understanding of colors, shapes, the lines of the face and body, texture, and lighting. Design methods for each makeup artist may differ, but can be broken down to who you're designing for, what look is needed to portray a certain idea, where are they going, how is the makeup used, and how can you execute each design accurately? During the design process for each new makeup look, you may be required to conduct research, go through an ideation process, create mockups and sketches, and finally, present your finished work.

Makeup artists often work with a design team made up of fashion designers, set dressers, photographers, directors, and more to create concepts and designs. Makeup artists have the option of taking classes to develop their skills or to begin working as a freelancer with friends and connections in the industry. If you choose to attend college, which is the preferred way to gain a foothold in this industry, you will take a variety of classes, which may include safety, skincare, hygiene, and sanitation; principles of makeup for beauty and fashion; corrective makeup techniques; makeup for broadcast and photography lighting; special effects and film makeup; and application techniques for lips, brows, and all-over body.

Makeup artists must work with different products, tools, textures, colors, shapes, and the human form to create each look. To excel in this field, a good sense of color theory is necessary to create the best color scheme for your clients' needs. Each makeup artist must have a firm grasp of the basics of color and an understand how lighting affects the appearance of color to the naked eye or through high-definition cameras that are often used within the industry. A solid understanding of color theory will better guarantee that you can make the right judgment call for each creative design, and ultimately, your customer.

With a strong understanding of color theory and the skill it takes to apply makeup to a human canvas, makeup artists can set themselves apart from a makeup applicator. Expert knowledge of different skin types, tool options, makeup products, the lines and shapes of the face, lighting, and application are all needed to succeed. After all, you may know color and have a grasp on the industry, but if you can't apply the makeup as requested, then you won't go far in this field.

GAIN EXPERIENCE & PROFESSIONAL CONNECTIONS

When pursuing a career as a professional makeup artist, it is important for beginners to build a strong portfolio, a personal brand, and industry connections. Building your portfolio, whether it is digital or in print, is a vital first step in building a career as a makeup artist. With a strong portfolio showcasing your work and growth, you are more likely to be accepted for an internship and book work within the industry. Include photos of makeup you've applied while working or volunteering at a local theater group, or on friends and family. Keep your portfolio fresh and up-to-date, as makeup techniques change, and you will be required to remain innovative and diverse in your skills. With modern advancements in communication and technology, it is more important than ever before to begin working on your own personal brand early on in your career. While it is always a good idea to let your finished work speak for your skill level, becoming recognized for your own personal style and flair can also be beneficial for jump-starting your career. Brand identity —whether you are utilizing social media or connections locally— is key to success. The professional makeup artistry field is extremely competitive and making connections within the industry via school, internships, or even personal relationships is indispensable to your future. While many new makeup artists are unsure of where to begin making these connections, it is always a good idea to practice by seeking out smaller jobs, possibly on a local or state level, to start building your reputation in the industry.

How to become a makeup artist. Top do's & don'ts

So you've been thinking about becoming a makeup artist so you can have a fun and exciting career. Good choice! So what's your next step? What kind of education do you need in order to become a professional makeup artist? How do you get your foot in the door so you can start working in your ideal dream job? The fact that there is no one direct path to working in the field of makeup artistry makes it necessary for you to check with your particular states make-up artists requirements.Now, depending on what it is exactly that you would like to do once you become an expert in makeup application will help you decide which of the many different career paths is going to be best for you. Know that no matter which career path you choose to take, there's a number of do's and don'ts that you should definitely follow if you want people to truly see you as a highly skilled makeup artist.

GENERAL ADVICE

You should seriously consider any job offer you receive when first starting out as a makeup artist, even if it's not your ideal job. It's highly likely that you're going to learn something of value with each and every job you accept, making it a good idea for you to be open to every new job opportunity. And think about all of the potential connections you can make. You should always be thinking about networking when working as a professional makeup artist.

And because your name is going to be directly tied to your business, it's essential for you to make sure that you leave a positive impression on everyone you come across in your industry.

DO'S & DON'TS

The following is a list of do's and don'ts for you to follow if you want to find success in the world of makeup artistry.

DO:

• Your homework. There are a number of different training and educational opportunities for potential makeup artists, and each and every state has their own requirements. The first thing you need to do is decide what it is exactly you want to do after you receive your make-up training. Do you want to apply makeup to celebrities? Do you want to work for a beauty salon? There are many opportunities available to you when working in this niche, making it necessary for you to figure out which path it is that you want to take.

• Share your secrets with others. Don't you want them to share their secrets with you? And when you think about it, is it truly a secret? Expert makeup artists have been applying makeup and using special application techniques for years now, so are there truly any new make-up secrets these days? It's really more a matter of finding a spin on how to apply makeup, which you should always share with your (trusted) peers.

• Know the trends! It's essential for you to be open to utilizing brand new makeup application techniques that are currently being used and/or tested.

• Use social media to promote yourself. This is one of the absolute best ways you can show people exactly who you are as a makeup artist. Remember to keep it professional!

• Always test the foundation shade on the side of your neck, not the inside of your wrist. Learning these types of makeup tips is going to take you far.

• Be friendly and approachable. Yes, even if you happen to be having a not so good day. When you're on the job it's essential for you to remain professional, and that includes being both pleasant and accessible.

• Trust your instincts. As time goes on, you're makeup application instincts will improve. If you're not sure about something, never hesitate to ask someone who has lots of makeup application experience.

• Consistently network with others. The more you're able to widen your list of contacts, the better off you are when it comes to knowing who's who. You never know where your next job is going to come from when you're a freelance makeup artist, so making new connections should always be on your list of things to do.

• Create a complete makeup portfolio. This should include a wide variety of your work so that others can get in all around understanding of who you are as a professional makeup artist.

DON'T:

• Apply makeup using bad lighting. Although most makeup artists agree that using natural daylight is the first choice, it's not always feasible. Using natural white light is a good choice, with LED lights becoming more popular in recent times. And remember, all overhead lighting is bad! Instead, you should focus the light so it's even with the client.

• Be negative. There's simply no room for negativity in the workplace, which can be a real time waster.

• Don't wait until the last minute to prepare for a new job. The last thing you want to happen is for you to appear unprepared to your new employer upon your first day arrival.

• Use poor quality beauty products. The line of beauty related makeup products you decide to use is directly going to represent who you are as a professional makeup artist. If you do decide to use lower quality beauty products, you're simply not going to be able to attract the high quality jobs that makeup professionals are seeking these days.

• Lie! Once you tell a lie, it's going to be very difficult for you to gain any trust back.

• Take short cuts. It's not worth the time or the money.

• Ignore any beauty related events that may be taking place in your area. Attending beauty events is a great way for you to expand your list of industry contacts.

• Buy any makeup until you've done your research.

A SUCCESSFUL MAKEUP ARTIST

Makeup artistry is a career that not everyone is brave enough to take. It is generally a rough path at the beginning, but don't be discouraged. There is enough opportunity for everyone wherever you may be situated. It is possible for you to become a remarkable makeup artist, if you just put your heart into it.

There are several ways you can approach the advancement of your career. Below are some means you should exert your effort into:

• Grab every opportunity you can to practice

• Build your portfolio

• Network with makeup artists and potential clients

• Keep in the loop on social media

• Consider attending a makeup school

PRACTICE MAKEUP ON FRIENDS AND FAMILY

Stretch your knowledge by practicing on friends and family. You may start with little to no pay but you will not regret all the lessons you are going to digest during this phase. It's the best time to experiment, create mistakes, and correct yourself. It's not only about grasping different makeup techniques, but it's also about learning how to deal with other people you call your clients.

Friends and family are your best bet if you're just starting out. They're the ones who will completely understand that you're still in the process of acquiring skills. They will support you in every way they can, which is actually very empowering to any individual whether you're looking to take makeup artistry as a career or not.

WORK ON YOUR PORTFOLIO

If there's one thing we cannot stress enough, it's for makeup artists to continuously update their portfolio. Every now and then, you will have different projects to work on, and what better way is there for you to take pride in your efforts than to showcase them?

It is highly recommended that you only include the best quality of photos, and there are important reasons why. As a makeup artist, you have to realize the essentials of a great portfolio. When considering how to become a successful makeup artist, know that high-quality imagery will help you lift your career and contribute to your advancement substantially. With professional-grade photography or video and a collection of showcased work in the bank whether that be made possible by your friends, family, peers, or other personal connections you'll have the fundamentals needed to pursue bigger, better projects.

CONNECT WITH FELLOW MUAS & TO THE MARKET

Never lose your connection with those who are in the same industry as you. Though it may be a competitive world out there, don't see others as a threat. Instead, you should set them as your inspiration to do your utmost best, because one day, you're going to need each other.If workshops, seminars, or any gatherings that allow you to network with others, take them. Never say no to such chances that will introduce you to potential clients who may later introduce you to more clients. If you're looking to become a makeup artist, perfecting your craft, while important, is one element; keep in touch with everyone you meet along the way.

LEARN HOW TO ADVERTISE YOUR SERVICE ON SOCIAL MEDIA

If you're absorbing advice and information on how to become a great makeup artist, you're doing yourself a disservice if you're not showcasing your work effectively! Part of this is leveraging social media and the internet at large. The best part? With time, management, and high-quality work, this relatively inexpensive avenue is a personality-driven bullhorn that gets your work out into the world with ease.Nowadays, everybody's on social media. A lot would look for their needs, including for MUAs, online, because it is easier that way. The convenience it brings is unbelievable, so that is one of the prime reasons why you should get in the trend of digital marketing. Put up a simple page where everybody can have access to your past works and see the magic work. Also put effort into disseminating information regarding your profile or website.

GET TRAINED AND RECEIVE A DIPLOMA FROM A MAKEUP SCHOOL

Nothing says trained than a hard-earned certificate. Employers and clients love MUAs who have had proper training because this means they can be trusted with their brushes and palettes. But besides appropriate learning, attending makeup school can be a fun experience.

ADDITIONAL TIPS ON HOW YOU CAN BECOME A MAKEUP ARTIST

From staying inspired to professional conduct, here are some things to know before your pursuit in becoming a makeup artist.

• Research makeup masters who inspire you: Take the time to determine what kind of look catches your eye and who your MUA role models are. You can begin by looking at magazines, websites, beauty vlogs, and public portfolios. Learn about your favorite MUA's backgrounds and paths to success, and, if applicable, follow suit. If you're wondering how to become a makeup artist for models, actors, and other high-profile individuals, your natural inclination may be to start here; but as your journey continues, never stop looking for ways to evolve your personal style and make the most out of the latest trends and iconic looks.

• Keep it professional. For many who want to learn how to become a makeup artist, working celebrities who are no stranger to the red carpet, billboard, or premier night is the ultimate goal. If you're fortunate enough to work with a star client, you must remain professional; after all, you're there to perform a service; and a poor interpersonal experience could tarnish a budding reputation or otherwise realign your professional trajectory.

• Bring your best attitude to every job. As you work your way up, take any job you can get to contribute to your portfolio and get experience — regardless of pay or perceived importance. You never know who you are going to meet, so it's crucial to stick to the golden rule; treat everyone the way you'd like to be treated.

• Find a mentor: Try to connect with a makeup artist who will let you tag along to their jobs. If you can wrangle working as their assistant or intern, even better! Forming a relationship with a mentor who can show you the ropes is an invaluable asset when starting out.

MORE STEPS TO BECOME A PROFESSIONAL MAKEUP ARTIST

In order to become a professional makeup artist, you have to follow the following steps. So, let's dive into the deep and explore the pathways of becoming a professional makeup artist.

CHOOSE YOUR NICHE

At the very first you have to do your homework and ask yourself some questions. As there are different types of training and educational opportunities for makeup artists, you need to decide what exactly you are going to do after you receive your makeup training.

Do you want to work in a salon or a beauty parlor for a recognized company? Or do you want to work for yourself? Do you want to apply makeup to celebrities or do you want to work in the theater?

PRACTICE HARD

As we all know practice makes perfect makeup artistry is no exception here. You can try different looks on yourself or your friends and family. The more you do the better you'll be.Experts suggest hands-on experience by working at a makeup counter at your local beauty salon. Try to find a mentor in your area who doesn't mind showing and giving you tips.

Your mentor will tell you to practice as much as you can. The more you practice with makeup the more comfortable you'll become. Also, you need to know about the products you are about to use on your clients.You can watch tutorials and videos to enrich your skills. Moreover, you need to practice every day and become confident to get your desired job.

GET FORMAL EDUCATION

As you are serious about becoming a professional makeup artist, formal education is a crying need.

First of all, you should choose a school that covers all aspects of applying professional cosmetics, including instructions on how to apply makeup for television and film, also fashion and beauty photoshoots, and magazine spreads.Choosing a school is very essential as it will help you with intense training and make you feel comfortable with receiving certification. Talk to your instructors about the best way to reach out to modeling agencies or television studios and make your network grow in this field.

Online learning also will be a great asset as they offer quality training with professional instructors. You have to invest your hours to gain such skills which will lead you to your dream and these certifications will certainly play a vital role.

CREATE A PORTFOLIO

You can find models to showcase your work. You necessarily don't need professional models, find the right people whose makeup you enjoy doing and whose faces are compatible with your style. Consider some Before and After photos of your models to include in your portfolio. Collaborations with other people will help to make your portfolio more attractive. Ask your friends and coworkers if she could use your makeup artistry services or offer to do wedding makeup.Meantime you'll hone your skills as well as start making a name for yourself. Don't hesitate to do some volunteer works at the beginning of your career. In the long run, you will be the ultimate winner. Taking some high-quality pictures of your work would definitely boost up your impression. Invest in a high-end camera or hire a photographer to take some picturesque pictures which will take your portfolio to another level.Visualization is very important in the makeup artistry industry. If you're looking to make a serious career you need to take these steps seriously. Your portfolio should reflect the brand you're creating. Your most creative and unique work should be showcased at the front so the clients should get an instant impression of your amazing talent. Include a range of specialties, from trendy fashion to old school, from special effects to television.

MARKET YOURSELF

After finishing your official training and creating a portfolio, you need to market your skills and services as much as you can. The internet is the best place to promote yourself as a professional makeup artist.You need to take advantage of the impact social media has on business marketing. You can start your social page and upload helpful short videos of performing specific makeup tasks.

Also, you can suggest products for different skin types and give professional tips to others. Once you have a valid social page of your own, clients are more likely to take you seriously.And you will reach many people as you will upload content regularly and make it easy for followers to get in touch with you. You may also want to start a YouTube channel where you can provide tutorials and show your skills to the world. Also, you can share your story of how you learned and improve your makeup skills.

Uploading videos of various techniques such as how to apply lashes, shape the brows with different tools, how to take care of your skin before and after makeup application will help you to get more followers.Once your channel gets popularity, different cosmetic and beauty brands may reach out to you, asking you to promote their products on your channel. Be sure to choose the right products that fit with the brand you've created as a makeup artist. And try the products yourself before recommending them to your followers. Always remember a bad product could hamper your reputation so quickly. Be honest to your follower and give authentic and informative tips which will help you to get loyal followers. You can also create an Instagram account and influence people about makeup. Linking your website, Instagram and YouTube channel will help you to grow your network and you can reach a bunch of people to help each other to grow.

BE PROFESSIONAL

As a makeup artist, your final goal is likely to get celebrity clients. You may be extremely excited to meet someone whose work you admire, remember to keep your coolness and remain professional.

There's time to talk to your client and tell that you're a fan but your objective should be to perform your job with precision and passion. As your reputation is on the line showing the highest professionalism would help you to get more star clients.

HOW TO BECOME A PROFESSIONAL MAKEUP ARTIST

Have you perfected the smokey eye? Can take one look at someone and whip out the perfect shade of lip liner? If so, you might be closer than you think to becoming a professional makeup artist. It takes skill, passion, and a whole lot of love for the assorted powders and creams, but you've got all that in spades. We'll fill you in on how to develop your skills, get experience, create a portfolio, and kick start your career. Just be sure that eyeliner is sharp before you get out there.

THINGS YOU SHOULD KNOW

- Practice at home by watching YouTube tutorials and doing your friends' makeup.

- Enroll in a cosmetology school or work at a cosmetics counter to get professional experience.

- Make up models and have them photographed to build your portfolio.

- Focus on a career path like the fashion industry, television, or freelance work.

DEVELOPING YOUR SKILLS

Study famous makeup vloggers on YouTube or Instagram: Online video tutorials can be an excellent (and free!) way to get started learning more about makeup artistry. Find makeup artists whose looks match the styles you're most interested in learning.

• Keep in mind that, while tutorials are a great starting point, there's no substitute for in-person training and experience.

Practice applying makeup on both yourself and your friends: This will help you develop your technique and perfect your craft. Remember that even though you may be a superstar at doing your own makeup, applying others' makeup takes a different set of motor skills and coordination.

• Apply makeup to people with different skin colors, face shapes, eye colors, and ages. This will help you develop the skills you need to work with a wide range of clients.

Begin to put together a "kit"—the brushes, makeup, and other tools you use regularly. These can be drugstore brands to start out. As you develop your career, you'll be able to afford more expensive products.

Familiarize yourself with current makeup trends: Read

magazines, scour fashion blogs, watch films, go to plays, and pay attention to the different trends and styles of face makeup. It is important to be up-to-date on current beauty trends so that you can advise clients.

• Clients may request that you recreate a certain look that a celebrity had at an awards show or in a magazine. You will need to learn the terminology involved in makeup artistry so that you can effectively bring your clients' descriptions to life.

GETTING EDUCATION AND PROFESSIONAL EXPERIENCE

Enroll in a makeup artist school that suits your schedule and budget: Since makeup artistry is not a licensed profession, states don't mandate course offerings from makeup artist programs—meaning that the curriculum varies widely between schools. Some schools offer full-time classes that cover all the bases, while others allow you to pick and choose courses that focus on particular industries or skills. These programs also vary widely in cost, with full-time schools being the most expensive.

• Typically, makeup training programs run 300-600 hours and can be completed in less than 6 months.

• Going to school is not a requirement for becoming a successful makeup artist. It may give you a boost in a very competitive field, however.

Find a job at a cosmetics counter to gain professional experience: Apply for positions at department stores or pharmacies. You'll have the opportunity to practice your skills on hundreds of people with different complexions, styles, and expectations. Best of all, you'll get paid to practice your skills.

• Retail experience is helpful for landing jobs in department and beauty stores, since your job will be selling cosmetics in addition to your makeup artistry services.

• Search for a company that is dedicated to training its employees in applying makeup, rather than focusing entirely on sales.

Join a local theater group to practice a different kind of makeup: Theater groups—at your school if you're a student, or in the wider community—are a great place to explore your creativity. You'll get a chance to practice a different style of makeup, learn to use greasepaint, and work with theatrical lighting.

Land an internship or apprenticeship with a respected makeup artist: Find a top makeup artist in your local area whose work you admire and ask if they would be willing to take on an apprentice or intern. Make it clear that you're eager to get real-world experience in the makeup industry.

• If they can't commit to an internship, ask if you can shadow them for a day or two. Even a few hours of observation could teach you tons of new techniques.

CREATING A PORTFOLIO

Find models to showcase your looks: While they don't have to be professional models, find people whose makeup you enjoy doing and whose faces are compatible with your style. Consider snapping some "before and after" photos of your models to include in your portfolio.

• Consider doing trade-for-print work with models.

Get creative with collaborations to build your portfolio: Ask your friend who's making a music video if she could use your makeup artistry services, or offer to do your coworker's wedding makeup. You'll hone your skills and start making a name for yourself at the same time.

• You may even need to volunteer your services in the beginning stages of your career to develop more content for your portfolio.

Take high-quality photographs of your work: Consider investing in a high-end camera or hire a photographer to help you put your portfolio together. The quality of the photographs can make or break a portfolio.

• If you're still early in your career, it's acceptable to take photos with your phone camera. Just make sure that your photos are well-lit and crisp.

Create a compelling portfolio that features all types of makeup styles: Your portfolio should reflect the brand you are creating. Your best, most creative work should be showcased at the front so prospective clients get an immediate impression of your unique talent. Include a range of makeup styles, from fashion to special effects to film and television.

• Your portfolio should exist both online and in print. The benefit of an online portfolio is that it reaches a larger audience and can be promoted through various forms of social media.

BUILDING YOUR CAREER

Focus on the fashion industry if you're good under pressure: Once you've gained basic education or professional experience (or both!), you'll need to determine what industry to focus on. Makeup artists who work in fashion are typically asked to employ their services at runway shows and fashion shoots.

• You may be called upon to work fast in stressful environments, like cramped backstage areas at fashion shows or outdoors in inclement weather during shoots.

• In this field, looks are led by the editor, designer, or fashion photographers rather than the makeup artist.

• You'll often work as part of a stylist and hair team to help prepare models.

Look for jobs in the television or film industry for a wide range of gigs: Most makeup artists are employed by the television and film industry, which offers a variety of opportunities in different styles of makeup. Applying makeup to a newscaster calls for a more natural look, while doing makeup on a sci-fi television show would require special effects work and a more imaginative style.

• Precision is important when working as a makeup artist in this industry. The crisper and clearer our television screens get, the easier it is to tell if someone's makeup isn't perfectly applied.

Freelance as a makeup artist for a more flexible work schedule: Many makeup artists build a lucrative career from freelance projects, moving from gig to gig with their kit in hand. People often hire makeup artists when preparing for photo shoots of bridal and wedding parties, family reunions, or graduations.

• Use word-of-mouth to promote your talents. Ask friends and family to consider hiring you to do their makeup for weddings, parties, or other formal occasions

Market yourself, particularly on social media: Whether you want to land a full-time job with a particular company or work as a freelancer on a project-by-project basis, start marketing yourself to get the word out that you're looking for makeup artistry work. Social media channels like Instagram and YouTube are very important, as well as a personal blog

TIPS TO BECOME A SUCCESSFUL MAKEUP ARTIST

Make-up is not just a hobby but is a form of art. A kind of art that enhances your physical beauty, yield confidence and whatnot. Who doesn't like to look good? Who doesn't want to feel confident? Have you ever fantasise to become chosen as a professional? Have you Wandered off in fantasy land about how to turn into a cool make-up artist? It's no big surprise. Getting paid to go throughout the day think about new trends, exploring different avenues regarding various looks, and working with cool customers is the thing that makes being a make-up artist a genuine dreamwork, yet like some other magnificent gig, it likewise takes a great deal of difficult work. How precisely do you go from lipstick addict to all-out blinking star? Here is the list of the most promising tips to become a successful make-up Artist:

GET ENROLLED IN A GOOD PLACE

If you are a beginner with a lot of enthusiasm or already know about how to do make-up, the first thing you need to do is to get under some experts hand. For a beginner, it works as a first ladder into this industry and for someone who already knows about makeup serve as a bridge to fill in all the gaps if there any left because of a desire to learn to make all the efforts. Learn about products, learn about techniques, skin type and everything that you require while practising.

PRACTICE

Practice plays an important role if you want to make a successful career in this profession. Like any other profession, it also requires a lot of practice. Practice is as important as learning. A great make-up artist is those who practice a lot. Practice is the key to ace in this industry. Practice with different products, skin type and facial shapes can boost your career in this profession.

FIGURE OUT THE BEST AND BAD

One of the key features of any professional field requires a deep understanding of oneself. If you want to become the best in this market, you should also know the area of strength and weaknesses. And after knowing the traits of the best and bad in you, start learning and exploring and practising those on different people to improve your chance of becoming a better make-up artist.

NETWORKING IS IMPORTANT

If you want to ace this industry with your tips and tricks. You require the right kind of networking. Use social media site, do publicised your work on different channels, attract more people. This industry is all about glamour and attractions and you need to glamourise your work to attract more customer. You can use Instagram, Facebook and especially YouTube to showcase your talent and if people love work online, they will gonna fetch you for more. The more you post, The more you grow is the formula of this industry.

LEARN THE NEW TREND

Everything Change with time and so does this industry. Every five years, the trend of fashion and makeup change. Though the basic remains same with time you need to unlearn the learn and learn the new trends. You need to learn and keep yourself up to date to match the need of the customers. You should do constant research and give the best what the customers are looking for because this is the industry of words and name and fame came to you with these words only. So learn the trends, keep yourself up to date and ready to serve the best.

ALWAYS HAVE YOUR SECRETS

Have you ever wonder why one makeup artist is famous over other although they use the same products. Just like the chef who has their secret ingredient and recipe similarly a professional make-up artist has their secret which he or she never share with anyone the secret help the makeup artist to grow audio over the other which keeps him in the long run. Space try to build up your secret and blow the mines off your customer with your techniques and tricks this will pave your ways to the top of this industry.

DON'T OVERDO IT!!

Any kind of makeup is done to enhance the beauty, physical features of our face and to feel confident so whenever you are doing make up try not to overdo it. keep a good balance of the product you are using and try to look as minimal as you can because the minimum is better than overdoing. so remember whenever you are practising or doing anyone's makes up try to enhance their real features rather than hiding them underneath.

RESPECT YOUR JOB

Love the job you are doing and try not to compare it with other professional jobs. Every profession has its pros and cons. Accept the pros of your profession and respect your client and try to give the best possible outcome of their choice. Communicate well and try to improve yourself with every suggestion rather than demotivating yourself !!!

9 7 9 8 8 6 2 7 7 2 5 0 0

Instagram e l'Incremento della Tua Popolarità: Strategie per il Successo

IncrementiOnline